967
OT

O'Toole, Thomas

Central African
Republic in pic

D0516559

CENTRAL
AFRICAN
REPUBLIC

...in Pictures

Visual Geography Series®

CENTRAL AFRICAN REPUBLIC

...in Pictures

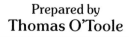

Prepared by
Thomas O'Toole

Lerner Publications Company
Minneapolis

17485

Courtesy of Tom O'Toole

A small truck makes its way over a flooded portion of the Trans-African Highway in the Central African Republic.

This is an all-new edition of the Visual Geography Series. Previous editions have been published by Sterling Publishing Company, New York City, and some of the original textual information has been retained. New photographs, maps, charts, captions, and updated information have been added. The text has been entirely reset in 10/12 Century Textbook.

LIBRARY OF CONGRESS CATALOGING-IN-PUBLICATION DATA

O'Toole, Thomas, 1941—
Central African Republic in pictures.

(Visual geography series)
Includes index.
Summary: Text and photographs introduce the geography, history, society, economy, and government of this central African country.
1. Central African Republic [1. Central African Republic] I. Title. II. Series: Visual geography series (Minneapolis, Minn.)
DT546.322.085   1989   967'.41   88-13588
ISBN 0-8225-1858-9

International Standard Book Number: 0-8225-1858-9
Library of Congress Catalog Card Number: 88-13588

VISUAL GEOGRAPHY SERIES®

Publisher
Harry Jonas Lerner
Associate Publisher
Nancy M. Campbell
Senior Editor
Mary M. Rodgers
Editor
Gretchen Bratvold
Assistant Editors
Dan Filbin
Kathleen S. Heidel
Photo Researcher
Karen A. Sirvaitis
Editorial/Photo Assistant
Marybeth Campbell
Consultants/Contributors
Thomas O'Toole
Sandra K. Davis
Designer
Jim Simondet
Cartographer
Carol F. Barrett
Indexer
Kristine S. Schubert
Production Manager
Richard J. Hannah

Photo by Barry Hewlett

Many Central Africans transport loads on their heads. This villager carries prepared food to a neighbor.

Acknowledgments

Title page photo courtesy of Tom O'Toole.

Elevation contours adapted from *The Times Atlas of the World,* seventh comprehensive edition (New York: Times Books, 1985).

1 2 3 4 5 6 7 8 9 10 98 97 96 95 94 93 92 91 90 89

Construction workers complete work on the roof of a community building in one of the nation's small towns.

Contents

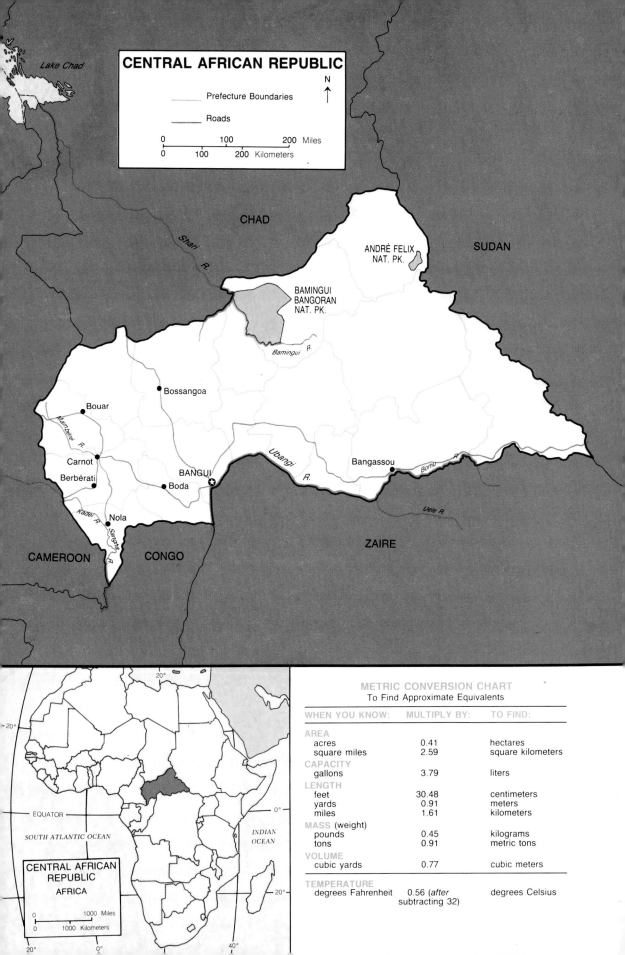

CENTRAL AFRICAN REPUBLIC

N

— Prefecture Boundaries

— Roads

| 0 | 100 | 200 | Miles |
| 0 | 100 | 200 | Kilometers |

CHAD

SUDAN

Shari R.

ANDRÉ FELIX
NAT. PK.

BAMINGUI
BANGORAN
NAT. PK.

Bamingui R.

Bossangoa

Bouar

Mambere R.

Carnot

Berbérati

BANGUI

Boda

Ubangi R.

Bangassou

Bomu R.

Kadei R.

Nola

Sangha R.

Uele R.

CAMEROON

CONGO

ZAIRE

Lake Chad

EQUATOR

SOUTH ATLANTIC OCEAN

INDIAN OCEAN

CENTRAL AFRICAN
REPUBLIC

AFRICA

| 0 | 1000 | Miles |
| 0 | 1000 | Kilometers |

METRIC CONVERSION CHART
To Find Approximate Equivalents

WHEN YOU KNOW:	MULTIPLY BY:	TO FIND:
AREA		
acres	0.41	hectares
square miles	2.59	square kilometers
CAPACITY		
gallons	3.79	liters
LENGTH		
feet	30.48	centimeters
yards	0.91	meters
miles	1.61	kilometers
MASS (weight)		
pounds	0.45	kilograms
tons	0.91	metric tons
VOLUME		
cubic yards	0.77	cubic meters
TEMPERATURE		
degrees Fahrenheit	0.56 (*after* subtracting 32)	degrees Celsius

Abounding with a great variety of plant and animal life, rain-forests grow in the southwestern part of the Central African Republic and along its main waterway—the Ubangi River.

Introduction

Independent since 1960, the Central African Republic occupies a region that includes savanna (grassland with scattered trees), several mountain ranges, dense rain-forests, and many rivers. Central Africans live in a landlocked country. This lack of access to oceans or seas presents a persistent barrier that hinders the Central African Republic's local economic growth and its participation in world trade.

The Central African population is composed of many ethnic groups—indeed, some estimates put the number at over 80. The histories of these groups are long but incompletely known. For example, evidence of human habitation in the region reaches back 8,000 years. Details, however, of what happened to the migrating groups as they settled into agricultural communities are still lacking.

Slave raids from the seventeenth century until the late nineteenth century took so many captives from the region that large areas of the country still suffer from a reduced population. To escape the slave traders, many Central Africans moved from place to place, avoiding contact with other peoples. The isolation between groups has contributed to the difficulty Central Africans have had in developing a national identity.

France gained control of the region in the late 1800s, naming its new colony Ubangi-Shari. European companies leased large tracts of land from the French colonial government. This arrangement changed the region's agricultural focus from small, food-growing farms to large

Workers and government officials observe the loading of bales of cotton prior to export from a new agricultural development. Europeans introduced cotton as a plantation crop in the early twentieth century.

Photo by *Africa Report*

A young Central African plays in a temporary camp set up by his roving clan in the rain-forest. Many of the nation's children, as well as its adults, live on a diet that does not have enough proteins or vitamins.

Photo by Barry Hewlett

A statue of Jean-Bedel Bokassa, former emperor of the nation, lies abandoned in Bangui. Bokassa's rule, which lasted from 1965 to 1979, was harsh for many Central Africans.

cotton, coffee, and tobacco plantations. Although the economy developed, the profits belonged to European investors. Central Africans remained poorly fed and inadequately housed, which increased the resentment against the colonial government.

Since gaining independence, the Central African Republic has maintained close links with France. The African nation receives significant amounts of financial aid each year and continues its relationship with many French investors. French remains the nation's official language, although only a small percentage of the population speaks it.

Since 1960 the nation has faltered under inefficient and often corrupt leadership. The level of production that some parts of the economy achieved in the early years of independence has been lost. Despite many promises of political freedom for Central Africans, government officials have abused their power. National leaders have postponed elections, have broken their own laws, and have taken financial advantage of their governmental positions.

Most Central Africans hope for strong, fair leadership to enhance national unity, to strengthen the economy, and to broaden political freedoms. In the late 1980s the nation was struggling to overcome its history of disrupted social development, as well as its economic disadvantage of being a landlocked nation.

This lake is located on the southern edge of the savanna – a region of grasses and scattered trees. Many lakes in the Central African Republic are seasonal, drying up after the rainy period ends.

1) The Land

The Central African Republic lies very near the middle of the African continent. It shares borders on the west with Cameroon, on the north with Chad, on the east with Sudan, and on the south with Zaire and Congo. Completely landlocked, the Central African Republic is over 375 miles from the nearest sea—the Gulf of Guinea on the Atlantic Ocean.

A large plateau, which is broken up by many rivers, covers most of the country. Mountainous regions fringe the plateau on the northeast and northwest. With 240,535 square miles of territory, the Central African Republic is slightly smaller than the state of Texas.

Topography

A large plateau, with an elevation of 2,000 to 3,000 feet above sea level, stretches across the middle of the Central African Republic. Only isolated *kaga* (granite peaks), occasional ridges, and river valleys break up the expanse of the plateau. Acting as a dividing point for the country's river systems, the plateau directs northern waterways into the Chad Basin and southern rivers into the Zaire (also known as the Congo) Basin.

The Yadé Massif mountain range, located on the northwestern frontier with Cameroon and Chad, is composed of kaga that vary greatly in height. Among them stands the nation's highest peak, Mount Ngaoui, which climbs to 4,658 feet above sea level. In the northeast, the Bongo mountain range rises along the nation's frontier with Sudan. Some peaks in this area reach over 4,000 feet in height. Large, diamond-rich formations of sandstone lie in the southwestern Central African Republic.

Rivers and Waterways

The Central African Republic has many rivers, which are branches of three main waterways. One system is the Shari River and its tributaries, which flow northward

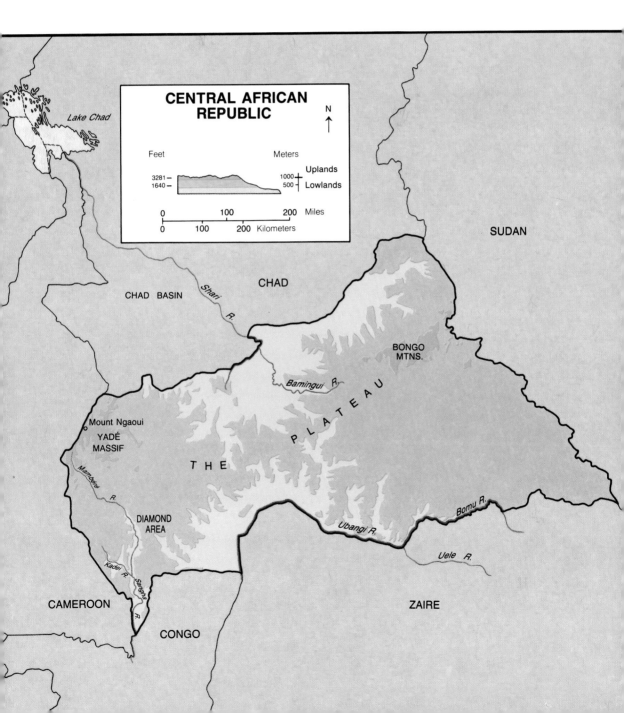

and empty into Lake Chad. This waterway system includes about one-third of the nation's rivers.

The Kadei and Mambéré rivers join south of the town of Berbérati to form the Sangha River, a second main waterway that drains about one-tenth of the country. This western river and its tributaries cut a 1,000-mile-long valley through western Africa.

The longest and most navigable river system in the region is the Ubangi, which covers 1,400 miles. It stems from the Bomu and the Uele rivers that begin in eastern Zaire. The Ubangi River flows westward from the town of Bangassou and traces most of the nation's border with Zaire. After passing through Bangui—the Central African Republic's capital—the river abruptly turns south and eventually travels into the Zaire Basin. Because it drains territory that receives heavy rains, the Ubangi carries a huge volume of water. At Bangui the river transports 33,000 cubic feet of water per second during the wet season.

Waterfalls on the country's many rivers offer opportunities for increased hydroelectric power—a goal the national government is pursuing in its economic development plans.

The Ubangi River is the Central African Republic's main waterway. Used extensively for transportation, the river is also a fishing ground for many Central Africans.

When seasonal rains arrive in May, they often fall rapidly in large quantities and cause flooding. Rains quickly swell the rivers – whose water levels sometimes rise several feet in a few hours.

Fishermen in a tributary of the Ubangi River playfully relax after taking in the day's catch.

Climate

Although the Central African Republic is located just over 300 miles north of the equator, the country does not register the extreme heat and humidity often measured in equatorial regions. Altitude and rainfall help to moderate the temperature, which ranges between 80° and 90° F most of the year. The country has three climate zones, and the territory becomes wetter and supports thicker vegetation in the southernmost zone.

The northern part of the country borders on the Sahel, an area between the Sahara Desert and more fertile areas to the south. This part of the Central African Republic has a six-month dry season, which occurs between November and April. During the remainder of the year, this portion of the country has a wet season in which about 30 inches of rain may fall. The extreme northeast, however, is the least-watered

13

A densely wooded area gives way to an area of widely scattered trees. In the rainy season the savanna is lush with vegetation, but when the rains end the trees turn brown and lose their leaves.

portion of the nation and is classified as semi-arid.

The large plateau that makes up most of the country receives more rain and has a shorter dry season than the northern zone. As much as 60 inches of rain may fall on the plateau during the wet months. Rainfall may be intense, with three to four inches of precipitation coming down in an hour. In this central climate area, temperatures during the dry season sometimes drop to 50° F at night.

The southern part of the country experiences the wettest climate, and the dry season is only a couple of months long. Some areas have no dry season at all. Seventy inches of rain fall each year within this climate zone. Sometimes the region's downpours raise river levels several feet in a few hours.

Flora and Fauna

Each climate zone supports vegetation suited to its rainfall level, temperature, and soil. In the arid northern region that borders the Sahel, very few varieties of plants can survive. Acacia trees produce gum arabic (a sticky material used in making candy and medicine). Shea trees also grow in this area, and their seeds produce an oil called shea butter, which is used in food, soap, and candles. Shrubs and tough grasses also thrive in the north.

Savanna—a region of grasses and trees —covers the central plateau. The variety of plants that grow on the savanna depends on the amount of moisture the region receives and the number of grazing animals it supports. Human inhabitants have altered the landscape by clearing it for farming.

Central Africans clear brush and trees from areas they want to farm by cutting and burning the foliage—a technique known as slash-and-burn.

A thick rain-forest lines the Ubangi River and covers portions of the southwestern corner of the country. The upper branches of trees that are as tall as 150 feet make a leafy canopy that shades the shrubs and vines growing at the lower levels of the forest. Many useful trees thrive in the area, including sapele mahogany and obeche.

Many varieties of flowering tropical plants flourish in the Central African Republic's rain-forests *(left)*. A flame tree *(below)* growing in a rural village shows its bright orange color when in full bloom.

Giraffes, antelope, buffalo, and elephants roam the northern and central regions of the Central African Republic, especially in Bamingui Bangoran and André Felix national parks. Predatory animals, such as lions, leopards, and cheetahs, also live on the savanna and in the forests.

Tsetse flies, which look like large houseflies, infest much of the country. The insect's bite transmits parasites that carry disease into the bloodstream of the bitten person or animal. Tsetse flies infect humans with sleeping sickness and cattle and horses with nagana, a deadly disease. The widespread presence of this pest has severely limited the development of settlements or farms in some areas of the country.

Courtesy of Tom O'Toole

The Central African Republic's tropical rain-forests contain many butterflies, which thrive in the area's moist climate.

Courtesy of Tom O'Toole

Green mangoes are among the tropical fruits most widely grown in the nation.

Courtesy of Peter Lodoen

Kicking its hind legs into the air, a young deer scrambles across a dirt road. Hunted as game animals, deer bring variety to the Central African diet, which tends to be high in starchy foods.

Elephants in the Central African Republic have dwindled from 80,000 in 1980 to fewer than 15,000 in the late 1980s. This sharp decline is due to poachers, who kill the elephants for their ivory tusks.

Leopards of the savanna blend with the colors of the trees in which they lie, often spotting their prey from the elevated vantage point. After catching an animal, leopards return to the tree branches to eat their kill.

Situated along the banks of the Ubangi River, the city of Bangui is the nation's capital and primary urban center.

Cities and Towns

Bangui, the capital of the Central African Republic, is the major urban area in the country and has a population of fewer than 400,000 people. Established by the French in 1889, the city's old section features wide, tree-shaded boulevards and a central market area, both of which reflect its colonial heritage. More modern sections of the city, furnished with electricity and running water, have developed to the north and west. Most Central Africans in Bangui, however, live in *kodros*—residential neighborhoods whose buildings are made of mud bricks with thatched roofs. Kodros receive no basic services (electricity, sanitation, and water) from the city government.

The western part of the nation hosts three of the Central African Republic's largest towns—Berbérati (population 93,000), Bouar (population 51,000), and

The cathedral in Bangui serves the Roman Catholic population of the capital and its surrounding region.

Some wealthy Central Africans have modern housing with electricity and running water.

Bossangoa (population 35,000). The population levels of these small cities vary widely from season to season, because many of the residents return to the countryside for long periods of time to farm or to hunt.

Many Central Africans live in small villages of fewer than 100 people. More than 6,000 of these settlements dot the countryside. Most of the villages are located in the southwestern Ubangi River Valley or in the northwestern highland area.

These workers are building the frame for a thatch roof, which will cover a home in one of the country's many villages.

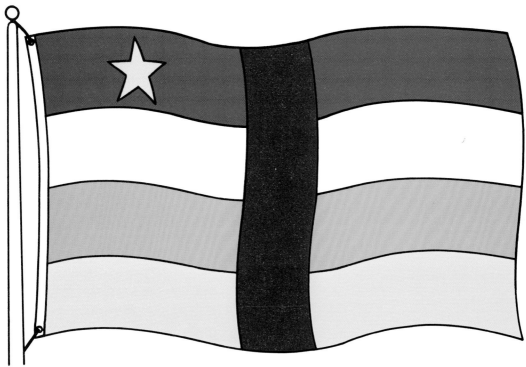

The flag of the Central African Republic includes the colors of Ubangi-Shari, Chad, Gabon, and Congo – the regions that made up the colonial territory known as French Equatorial Africa. The Central African Republic originated from the colony of Ubangi-Shari.

2) History and Government

Archaeological evidence reveals that people inhabited the territory of the Central African Republic as long as 8,000 years ago. The population lived in small groups that shifted their campsites from time to time in search of a better food supply. The scarcity of food forced each community to seek advantages over its neighbors. Groups rarely united with one another or developed fixed settlements, and the population's growth rate remained low. Much later, slave raids disrupted those settlements that did exist and reduced their populations.

Early History

Diamond miners in the twentieth century discovered polished flint and quartz tools that were made around 6000 B.C. in central Africa. Archaeologists have determined that the residents who made these tools survived by hunting animals and by gathering edible plants. Beginning in about 1000 B.C., the inhabitants cleared sections of the thick, dry forest that covered most of the middle of the Central African Republic and planted grains such as millet and sorghum on small plots of land. By 500 B.C. the area took on the characteristics of the savanna that now stretches across the Central African plateau.

In about 500 B.C. local farming people in the western portion of the country, near present-day Bouar, carefully arranged stone monuments weighing several tons. The cooperation necessary to make and to position these monuments suggests that the farming groups responsible for the stones had achieved a large measure of social organization and unity. Scholars know little else, however, about the people of this time. Stone tools—the next evidence of the inhabitants of the region—have been found along the Mbomu and Shari rivers and date from A.D. 1000.

The speech patterns of modern Central Africans belong to the Central Sudanic and Ubangian language families. In A.D. 1400, ethnic groups speaking these tongues lived in isolated settlements and operated independently of one another.

By this time iron tools were common, and farmers regularly cut down trees and burned them (the slash-and-burn method) in order to clear land for planting. Drought often destroyed crops, and tsetse flies infected animals with deadly diseases, making livestock difficult to raise. Scarcity of food caused conflict among groups of Central Africans as they competed for better farmland and for greater access to game animals.

During the fifteenth and sixteenth centuries, accounts of kingdoms that had developed in the region appeared in written records in Europe and the Middle East. The reports, many of them considered legendary by modern historians, give little concrete information of these settlements beyond their names—Goaga, Anzica, and Aloa.

Until the seventeenth century, the region of the Central African Republic was

By 500 B.C., farmers in the middle of what is now the Central African Republic had cleared much of the forest land, and gradually the region became permanent savanna.

not directly connected to any of the main commercial routes that extended through Africa to Europe and to Asia. But, by the beginning of the seventeenth century, Arab slave traders had begun to extend the trans-Saharan and Nile River trade routes into the region.

The Slave Trade Develops

Although Africans had occasionally been taken from the region as slaves before the first century A.D., the slave trade became a regular activity from the seventeenth to the middle of the nineteenth century. Arab and African traders captured people and sent them as slaves to North Africa or to the Atlantic coast. From these points, slave ships transported the captives to the Americas or to Asian markets.

In the early seventeenth century the small, northern Islamic states of Bagirmi, Wadai, and Darfur began to raid the Sara, Banda, and Mboum peoples that lived within the region of what is now the Central African Republic. On some occasions Islamic slave traders offered guns, cloth, jewelry, or food in exchange for captives, but usually no payment was made.

By the mid-nineteenth century, the Bobangi people from the Ubangi River area had become slave traders themselves and

Courtesy of Schomberg Collection, New York Public Library

Beginning in the seventeenth century, North African and Arab traders kidnapped many people living in the region of the Central African Republic. After transporting the captives across the Sahara Desert, the traders sold them into slavery.

Local people shipped captives in large canoes down the Ubangi and Zaire rivers to the Atlantic coast. The traders then turned these new slaves over to brokers, who transported them in ships across the ocean and sold the slaves in the colonies of the New World.

raided the nearby Gbaya and Manja peoples. The new slaves were transported to the Atlantic coast, where they were handed over to slave brokers who sold the captives in overseas markets.

The slave trade disrupted the development of social unity among the region's ethnic groups. Deep resentments against the raiding groups grew. (Indeed, anger continues to surface in present-day inter-ethnic relations.) Raiders not only stole people from their homes but also unknowingly introduced new diseases into the area. Central Africans were not immune to these new viruses, and many died from smallpox, measles, and other illnesses.

Hoping to avoid capture, Central Africans fled from their homes, and entire groups would sometimes migrate from one area to another. They were especially watchful during the dry season, when slave raiders were most active because they could travel more easily.

This constant upheaval hampered the development of strong social organizations among the region's ethnic groups. Villages remained isolated from each other as the waves of raiders met the increasing demand for slaves in other parts of the world. Large areas of the Central African Republic still have sparse populations as a result of the loss of so many people during the slave-trading era.

Expanding Commercial Trade

The slave trade brought the region into direct contact with major African trade routes. In the eastern part of the country, markets gradually developed. A few Arab traders came into the area in the early eighteenth century to exchange their tea,

Central Africans who were sold into the Atlantic slave trade often worked on large plantations—tending, harvesting, and processing sugarcane, tobacco, or cotton. A period drawing illustrates a sugar mill in seventeenth-century Brazil, where many slaves from the region of the Central African Republic were sent.

Independent Picture Service

Independent Picture Service

In an eighteenth-century drawing, African and European slave traders work out the details of buying and selling the captives that stand in a circle around them. The Europeans' payment of rum and guns lies piled on the ground in a fort built by the Danish in the territory of present-day Ghana. African brokers were skillful at negotiating, and they were often fiercely competitive with one another.

sugar, cloth, salt, and perfume for the ivory that the local inhabitants had taken from elephants they had killed. The Arabs also brought seeds and cuttings for new crops, such as maize (corn) and cassava (a root crop)—both of which grew easily and plentifully in the Central African soil.

These new sources of food and income increased opportunities for Central African groups to organize into social and political units. Gradually, small kingdoms of the Azande and Ngbandi people emerged in the area of the eastern Central African Republic.

By the end of the nineteenth century, the growing economy in the eastern territory had attracted European merchants to seek closer ties with the region. They hoped to gain access to the raw materials that the Africans in this area had begun to gather. The Europeans also wanted to establish markets for their goods.

The Ubangi-Shari Colony

In the last decades of the nineteenth century, fast ships, powerful weapons, and quinine—a medicine that helps control malaria—made it possible for Europeans to gain control of vast areas of Africa. The industrial revolution in Europe had created the need for more markets and for new sources of raw materials. Most Europeans felt that the region of the Central African Republic filled neither of these roles. The French government, however, began to regard the territory as a way to reach the rich areas of both the Nile River Valley and Lake Chad.

European powers—including Belgium, Germany, Britain, and France—competed for control of African territories that previously had been unclaimed as colonies. French colonists arrived in what is now the Central African Republic in the late 1880s. They named the area Ubangi-Shari, after

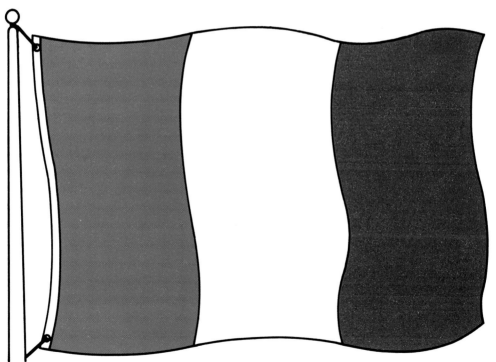

Artwork by Jim Simondet

The French flag flew over Ubangi-Shari in 1910, when the territory joined Gabon, Congo, and Chad as part of French Equatorial Africa.

the two major river systems they found there.

In conferences held in Europe at the end of the nineteenth century, the European powers worked out boundaries for Ubangi-Shari and other territories. By the beginning of the twentieth century, colonial frontiers had been set for western and central Africa without consulting the local people. In 1910 the French added Ubangi-Shari to Gabon, Congo, and Chad, creating the federation of French Equatorial Africa. Although a governor-general ruled the entire federation, a lieutenant governor, who lived in Bangui, had authority in Ubangi-Shari.

The Africans living in the colony did not want to submit to French control. Consequently, the French used military force in the early years of the twentieth century to subdue the African people. Nevertheless, Baram-Bakié, an African leader from the Vridi group, continued to maintain control of a small portion of territory near the Ubangi River from 1905 to 1910. Although other African villages also attempted to remain independent, the French army eventually overcame them.

Courtesy of Tom O'Toole

This monument marks the farthest point reached by French adventurer Alfred Fourneau, who explored the region that would become the Central African Republic.

Photo by Marty Schneider

European overseers forced Africans to hunt and kill more and more elephants for their ivory tusks. The frequent slaughter caused a sharp decline in the elephant population.

The Effects of Colonization

After it had established control in the region, the French government profited from the colony by leasing large tracts of land to private European companies. Upon gaining a lease, a firm had almost complete power to administer the land as it desired. Company overseers forced Central Africans —often by means of physical punishment —to gather the wild rubber that grew on the land and to sell their ivory to foreign merchants. During this same time, famine and disease drastically reduced the quality of life for African peoples. In addition, family farms were absorbed into larger plantations—a development that caused further breakdowns in village life.

European politics determined many colonial borders during the early twentieth century. As a result, portions of Ubangi-Shari were sometimes administered as part of Congo or Cameroon, and different European powers controlled areas of the Ubangi-Shari colony for various periods of time. A western region called Neu Kamerun (New Cameroon), for example, was in German hands from 1911 to 1914.

In the 1920s the French government forced thousands of men from Ubangi-Shari to work on the Congo-Ocean Railroad, which was being built in the French colony of Congo, hundreds of miles from their homes. Central Africans again refused to submit to forced labor and staged several uprisings, which French troops quickly put down.

The region experienced little social, political, or educational development in the first decades of the twentieth century. In the late 1920s, the French began to create a mobile health system in the colony to fight disease—especially sleeping sickness. Other improvements occurred as a result of the arrival of Roman Catholic

27

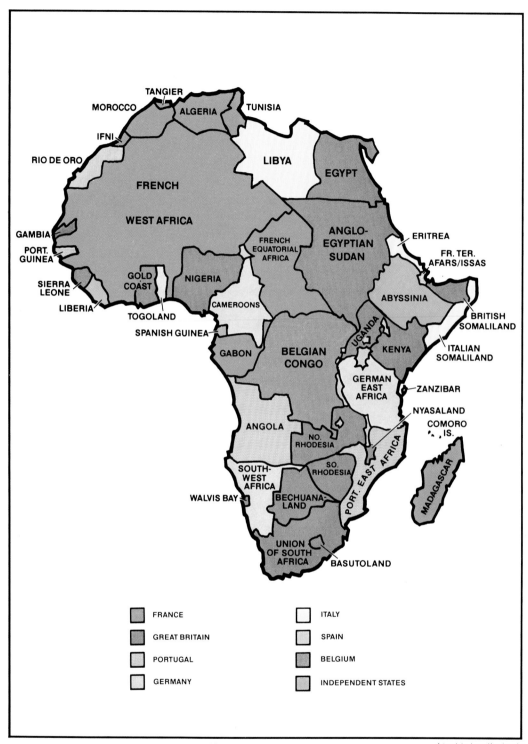

TANGIER

MOROCCO ALGERIA TUNISIA

IFNI

RIO DE ORO

FRENCH

WEST AFRICA

LIBYA

EGYPT

GAMBIA

PORT.
GUINEA

SIERRA
LEONE

LIBERIA

GOLD
COAST

TOGOLAND

SPANISH GUINEA

NIGERIA

FRENCH
EQUATORIAL
AFRICA

CAMEROONS

GABON

ANGLO-
EGYPTIAN
SUDAN

ERITREA

FR. TER.
AFARS/ISSAS

ABYSSINIA

BRITISH
SOMALILAND

ITALIAN
SOMALILAND

UGANDA

KENYA

BELGIAN
CONGO

GERMAN
EAST
AFRICA

ZANZIBAR

NYASALAND

COMORO
IS.

ANGOLA

NO.
RHODESIA

SOUTH-
WEST
AFRICA

SO.
RHODESIA

MADAGASCAR

PORT. EAST AFRICA

WALVIS BAY

BECHUANA-
LAND

UNION
OF SOUTH
AFRICA

BASUTOLAND

FRANCE

GREAT BRITAIN

PORTUGAL

GERMANY

ITALY

SPAIN

BELGIUM

INDEPENDENT STATES

Artwork by Larry Kaushansky

European governments had carved Africa into areas of influence by the late nineteenth century. The southern part of French Equatorial Africa and a bit of eastern Cameroons became the Central African Republic in 1960. Map information taken from *The Anchor Atlas of World History*, 1978.

Christian missionaries who arrived in the Central African Republic in the years prior to World War II founded this Catholic church at Mbaiki.

and Protestant missionaries, who set up schools and medical clinics.

The French attempted to make the colony more profitable in the mid-1930s. Their plan to force African farmers to grow cotton, however, did not bring the immediate increases of revenue that the French had expected. Coffee plantations might have been productive, but a crop disease destroyed many of the coffee trees in 1938. Only a gradual increase in gold and diamond production brought profit to French investors.

The Aftermath of World War II

When Germany took over France during World War II (1939–1945), French general Charles de Gaulle called for the help of French troops, European colonists, and residents of the colonies. Three thousand Central Africans fought on the side of the French in battles in North Africa, the Middle East, and Europe. After the war, many Gbaya, Manja, and Banda troops returned

General Charles de Gaulle issued an urgent call to residents of French territories for help in fighting against Germany during World War II. Three thousand Central Africans responded and fought on the French side during the global conflict.

29

to their homeland with a sense of national identity. They no longer regarded themselves only as members of separate ethnic communities. These war veterans had a wide awareness of the world and of the possibilities for their own region.

In the late 1940s, the colony prospered under Governor-general Felix Eboué, a West Indian appointed by de Gaulle—the head of state in France. Eboué had served in different positions within the Central African Republic for 20 years before assuming his high post. To give some authority to local people, he sought out African leaders and named them as administrators in the region.

With financial assistance from the United States, the French government launched a series of public projects in Ubangi-Shari. These improvements, along with increased investment in mining, led many to think that progress might occur in the colony. But since few Central Africans could afford to buy the products that other Central Africans created, individual African farmers and workers had little motivation to manufacture surplus goods. Demands on the world market for Ubangi-Shari products grew slowly, and only a few French settlers had enough money to invest in factories or in big farms.

In return for African help during the war, de Gaulle began reforming the way in which France ran its African colonies. In 1946 de Gaulle organized French holdings into a cooperative political association called the French Union. De Gaulle created new local assemblies, and French colonists and some Africans became regional political representatives. A few Africans even participated in the national assembly of France.

At first, the French granted rights in the newly established French Union to only a few educated Africans. As time passed, however, more and more Africans gained the right to vote. On November 10, 1946, Barthélémy Boganda became the first Central African elected to the French legislature.

Barthélémy Boganda left the Roman Catholic priesthood to work for his nation's independence. In 1957 he became the first president of the new Ubangi-Shari Territorial Assembly. This monument in Bangui commemorates Boganda's efforts on behalf of Central African independence.

Barthélémy Boganda

A French-educated Roman Catholic priest, Barthélémy Boganda worked for reform within the French Union rather than for national independence. After petitioning to leave the priesthood, Boganda was free in 1949 to form the Movement for the Social Evolution of Black Africa—known by the French abbreviation, MESAN. As a political party, MESAN united many Central Africans who were dissatisfied with French rule.

Boganda helped Central Africans overcome the forced-labor practices they endured under the cotton producers and coffee plantation owners. He also introduced legislation in the national assembly in France to end ethnic discrimination in the territory's legal system and to decrease taxes that Africans had to pay. The goals of Boganda and MESAN included securing basic rights for the people in Ubangi-Shari. Although national independence was only a distant objective, Boganda's efforts distressed the French colonists, who feared MESAN's efforts to change the system of government.

The Loi Cadre (basic law), which was passed in France in 1956, eliminated the final barriers to full voter participation in the territories. It also created government structures to help the colonies to develop self-rule. Boganda and MESAN were so popular with Africans that the party won all the seats in the 1957 election. Boganda became president of the newly formed Ubangi-Shari Territorial Assembly.

The Road to Independence

The French government wanted the members of the French Union to evolve into a community of independent territories, with France as their leader. France looked to MESAN, headed by Boganda, as the logical group to lead Ubangi-Shari to independence within such an organization.

In September 1958, the French dissolved French Equatorial Africa and increased

Photo by Barry Hewlett

A young Mbaka man prepares to start another day of harvest. A generation ago, Barthélémy Boganda founded MESAN to change the forced-labor practices under which Central Africans had worked and to reform the French systems of law and taxation.

the authority of the individual territorial assemblies. These governing bodies now handled duties that dealt with all the internal affairs for their particular regions. France still controlled the territories' foreign relations. In December 1958 changes in the French constitution transformed the French Union into the French Community and allowed the territories even more self-rule.

Boganda hoped that the former French territories of Chad, Gabon, Congo, and Ubangi-Shari could form a single nation. He had visions of an even larger grouping—the United States of Latin Africa—which would also include Zaire, Angola, and Cameroon. Boganda feared that landlocked Ubangi-Shari would have many economic difficulties if it became a separate country. Still desiring to keep the individual territories somewhat dependent on France, de Gaulle and the French government did not support Boganda's unification plans. When Gabon, Chad, and Congo rejected the plan

31

to unify, Boganda led Ubangi-Shari to accept the new constitution offered by France.

Boganda died in a plane crash on March 29, 1959. The territorial assembly chose David Dacko, a former schoolteacher, to replace Boganda as president, selecting him over Boganda's longtime assistant Abel Goumba. The Central African Republic achieved independence on August 13, 1960, when the French delegate, André Malraux, signed agreements between the French national assembly and the Ubangi-Shari national legislature.

Dacko and Bokassa

After the Central African Republic achieved independence, Dacko and a small group of French-supported Central Africans gained complete power in the new nation. Abel Goumba and a handful of his followers objected to Dacko's takeover. Goumba soon began MEDAC, a rival party to MESAN, and the police arrested him. After Dacko discredited MEDAC through a series of false charges, he assumed the presidency without a formal election and without further opposition.

Although the Central African Republic was independent, Dacko made international agreements that gave France broad authority in trade, defense, and foreign relations. In other governmental areas, French officials were paired with Central Africans, who hoped to increase their participation in government, but this dual administrative approach was ineffective. Government positions multiplied, and the increased number of salaries drained the national budget. Government officials began spending less money on roads and other necessities while they accumulated debts for luxury cars, foreign travel, and unneeded equipment.

In 1962 Dacko named MESAN, which by then he controlled completely, as the only national political party. During elections held in early 1964, Dacko ran unopposed and again became president. A few months later the MESAN candidates won all 60 seats in the elections for the national assembly.

The economy grew weaker and the national debt grew larger during Dacko's rule. On December 31, 1965—amid impending bankruptcy and a threatened countrywide strike—the commander of the

The Central African imperial standard (banner)—flown during Bokassa's coronation ceremonies and at his palace—had a field of green because it was the favorite color of both Bokassa and his hero—Napoleon Bonaparte.

Artwork by Jim Simondet

A large, bronze statue of Jean-Bedel Bokassa lies on the ground near his palace. Now in decay, the palace was Bokassa's headquarters until 1979, when David Dacko took over the government for the second time.

army, Jean-Bedel Bokassa, replaced Dacko through a coup d'état (a swift, forceful overthrow of a government).

Bokassa took over all important governmental positions, defeating opposition wherever it formed. He suspended the nation's constitution and dissolved the legislature. He often took a direct part in crushing opposition by assisting the police and army as they arrested, questioned, and sometimes beat prisoners.

Despite Bokassa's increasingly harsh style of government, France continued to support him and the faltering economy. The French wanted to retain access to the country's diamond mines and to its potential uranium supply. French paratroopers were sent to the Central African Republic in the mid-1970s to help bolster Bokassa's rule.

To keep Bokassa in power, France negotiated loans from the Republic of South Africa and from private banks in the United States. France gave assurances that the Central African Republic would pay back the loans and pointed to the country's mineral resources as proof of its financial security.

Bokassa's Central African Empire

In 1976 Bokassa proclaimed himself emperor of the nation, which he renamed the Central African Empire. The crowning took place in December 1977, and the French government financed and organized much of the costly coronation ceremonies. Almost one-half of the annual income of the Central African Empire was spent on Bokassa's imperial ceremony. Many Central Africans saw their already low income—which had never been more than several hundred dollars a year per person—decline even more.

Under Bokassa's rule, the government went further into debt. The emperor rewarded those who supported him by giving them government positions and by increasing the salaries of those he already employed. Bokassa personally administered the nation's diamond trade and took most of the profits for himself. The cost of consumer goods rose, and the quality of basic services declined. The nation's economy depended increasingly on financial aid from France.

In January 1979, Bokassa ordered all high school students to wear uniforms

33

made in one of his factories. This led to student demonstrations in Bangui against the emperor, who called out the army to subdue the crowd. During street fighting, over 100 students and their supporters died.

A panel of Central African judges charged Bokassa with murder. Spurred by this development, France decided to overthrow Bokassa's government in September 1979 and abruptly halted aid to the empire. Bokassa responded by flying to Libya to ask for assistance from Moammar Kadafi—the Libyan head of state and France's enemy. The French quickly flew former president Dacko from Europe into Bangui, along with French troops from Gabon and Chad. Within hours this French-backed coup had deposed Emperor Bokassa, and soon the country changed its name back to the Central African Republic.

Bokassa eventually flew to France and requested political protection as a French citizen. The French refused to let him leave the plane and sent him instead to Côte d'Ivoire (formerly Ivory Coast) in West Africa. The French later allowed Bokassa to enter France. When Bokassa returned to the Central African Republic in 1986 to try to gain popular support, he was arrested. At a public trial in 1987, a court found him guilty of murder, embezzlement (stealing), and other crimes. In 1988 Bokassa's death sentence was reduced to life imprisonment.

Dacko's Second Government

Dacko's second turn at governmental control, which began in September 1979, was not received with enthusiasm. To maintain his power, Dacko relied on French paratroopers and on administrative officials

Army troops escort former Central African emperor Jean-Bedel Bokassa into the courtroom at the start of his trial in 1987 for murder and other crimes. The court found Bokassa guilty. Later his death sentence was changed to to life imprisonment.

Crowds throng to a commemorative site dedicated to Barthélémy Boganda—the first Central African elected to the French legislature and the founder of the Central African Republic.

from Bokassa's government. Active opposition to Dacko's rule arose as secondary school students and unemployed urban dwellers demonstrated in Bangui.

France pressured Dacko to give some sign of efforts to increase democratic processes. In response, Dacko called for a new constitution and held elections in early 1981. Dacko won the election, but government interference and obvious vote fraud caused many Central Africans to doubt that the results were accurate.

Labor strikes and bomb attacks undermined Dacko's control of the country, and changes within the French government weakened support from abroad. Dacko increasingly began to rely on the army to keep his government in power. On September 1, 1981, General André Kolingba, a member of the Yakoma people, removed Dacko from office by a coup and established a military government.

Two soldiers of the Central African Republic stand guard during ceremonies at the Boganda memorial.

35

The Martin Luther King Center in Bangui opened in the summer of 1986. Soldiers from the Central African Republic join in the dedication of the U.S.-sponsored social service center.

Kolingba's Rule

Upon taking control of the Central African Republic, Kolingba stated that he would try both to strengthen the economy and to establish a democratic government. In an attempt to stabilize the economy, Kolingba requested huge amounts of aid from neighboring African states and from France. The French government responded by continuing the large loans and subsidies that it had customarily given to the country.

Kolingba also promised to stamp out governmental corruption and to reduce the overlarge civil service.

Many of the civil servants from Bokassa's and Dacko's administrations remained, however, and corruption grew rather than diminished. In addition, despite his promise to establish democracy, Kolingba delayed elections year after year. Ange Patassé—a popular political figure from a small ethnic group in the northwest—challenged Ko-

One of the highways slated for improvement, National Route One near Bouar is a main thoroughfare in the nation's network of roads. Of 13,300 miles of roads, only about 400 miles are paved.

lingba's rule in the spring of 1982. But Patassé's political activities endangered him, and he eventually fled the country under French protection.

The Central African government stayed almost entirely in the hands of the military until 1985. In that year Kolingba dissolved the military committee, which had ruled the country since 1981, and named a new 25-member cabinet that included a few civilians. In early 1986, under pressure from the World Bank and other international organizations, Kolingba formed a committee to increase gradually the level of democratic participation. The government, however, continued to operate under the direct control of Kolingba.

In November 1986 the Central African government sponsored a referendum asking the voters to extend Kolingba's rule for six years and to approve a new constitution. The people approved both of these measures by a large majority, but many questioned the results. After the referendum, the government of the Central African Republic remained in the hands of Kolingba.

Government

The constitution of the Central African Republic was suspended when André Kolingba took control of the government in 1981. Although the national assembly approved a new constitution in 1986, it was not put into effect. The executive branch is composed of a president and a cabinet, with individual cabinet members representing each district of the country.

Kolingba also suspended the legislature in 1981. As president, he holds all executive and legislative power in the nation, and the judicial branch lacks the freedom to challenge his direction. The highest court in the nation is the supreme court, with appeals courts, criminal courts, and lower courts making up the rest of the judicial system.

Photo by Barry Hewlett

Bangui—the capital city and governmental center of the Central African Republic—is situated on the Ubangi River.

Central African children eat fruit as they play in their village. Almost half of the country's population is under 15 years of age.

Photo by Barry Hewlett

3) The People

With only 2.8 million people, the Central African Republic is a sparsely populated country. Averaging 11 people per square mile, the population is distributed very unevenly, with high concentrations of Central Africans in settlements along the Ubangi River and near the borders with Chad and Cameroon.

Like most other African nations, the Central African Republic has a large rural population, with roughly 65 percent of its people residing in the countryside. Forty-three percent of Central Africans are below the age of fifteen. The large percentage of young people in the Central African Republic is due to the country's high birth

38

A girl from a rural community carries her brother in a sling on her back. As they go about their daily business, many Central African women carry their children or siblings in this way.

Most of the nation's people have a connection to the land, even if they live in a city or town. Several grown members of the family who own this farm in Western Central African Republic have emmigrated to Banqui, but during planting and harvesting time they return to work in the fields.

rate. Life expectancy in the nation is 45 years—one of the shortest average life spans on the African continent.

Ethnic Groups and Languages

Estimates of the number of ethnic groups residing within the Central African Republic vary from 30 to over 80. Identifying the number of members in each group is difficult because the people often link census taking with taxation or with forced-labor programs. Consequently, many members of the nation's ethnic groups avoid being counted.

The ethnic groups of the Central African Republic can be categorized by their geographic region. Most groups reside either in a river region or in savanna territory. The various Central African peoples can also be grouped according to the languages they speak. The most prominent river groups are the Yakoma, the Sango, and the Mbaka. The political leaders Barthélémy Boganda, David Dacko, and Jean-Bedel

Courtesy of Peter Lodoen

In rural areas, the roofs of homes and farm buildings are made of thatch or straw. The savanna surrounding this village has great agricultural potential.

Courtesy of Tom O'Toole

Many Central African ethnic groups rely on the nation's rivers for their livelihoods. These fishermen have set up a temporary dwelling on a riverbank to provide a place of rest from their travels.

Accompanying an Aka dancer, another member of the Aka ethnic group sits in front of his home and plays a traditional African stringed instrument.

Bokassa are from this last group. The Central African Republic's president, André Kolingba, comes from the Yakoma group. The savanna peoples include the Banda—the largest of all the groups—the Gbaya, the Sara, and the Manja.

All of the river groups and some of the savanna groups speak languages that belong to the Ubangian language family. Historians know that people speaking these languages came to the region before A.D. 1000. Coming into the region from the area of present-day Cameroon and Congo, Ubangi-speakers spread from the southwestern corner of the Central African Republic into the rest of the country. Sango—a Ubangian tongue named after the ethnic group that first spoke it—became the language of trade for many of the peoples along the rivers. When France colonized the region, they used Sango as they traveled through the territory, thus carrying the influence of Sango even farther.

Some savanna groups, such as the Sara, use languages that belong to the Central Sudanic family. This language family probably entered the region from Sudan around A.D. 1000. Most speakers of Central Sudanic languages reside in the northern and eastern parts of the country.

More and more Central Africans are migrating to Bangui and adapting to an urban way of life.

41

One notable ethnic group that cannot easily be classified either by region or speech is the Aka. A people of small physical stature—sometimes no more than four feet tall—the Aka are well adapted to move quickly and easily through their traditional lands in the southwestern rainforests. These people make new dwellings as they travel from place to place searching for edible plants and game animals.

Because of the Central African Republic's colonial heritage, French has become the official language of the country, even though less than 10 percent of the people speak it. Sango is the actual national language, spoken by almost everyone in the land.

Daily Life

Most Central Africans, including a large number of urban dwellers, continue to live off the land. They practice age-old agricultural techniques and have little money with which to make farming improvements. Central Africans remain unable to raise enough nutritious food to feed their families.

Photo by Barry Hewlett

An Aka man stands in front of his dwelling with his hunting spear. The Aka depend upon catching small game animals in the rain-forest for much of their food supply.

Most Central Africans launder their clothes on the banks of streams, spreading their garments out on the ground to dry in the sunlight. Often with babies strapped

Courtesy of Tom O'Toole

These horned zebu are valuable to the herders who raise them. The cattle are sold for high prices when they are brought to market.

to their backs, rural women work throughout the day. They transport loads of firewood or containers of water on their heads. Women also grow the bulk of the nation's food. Most of the men cultivate crops that will be exported—such as coffee, cotton, and tobacco—or they hunt and fish to supply food.

A small number of wealthy Central Africans live in Bangui or one of the nation's few regional towns. They engage in business enterprises that are often controlled by non-African investors. Central Africans who can afford the expense often choose to send their children to school in France.

Courtesy of Tom O'Toole

Courtesy of American Lutheran Church

Rivers not only provide transportation and food but also give nearby villagers a place to wash their clothes (above). A woman (left) from a rural area carries a mud brick of the kind from which most Central African houses are made.

Courtesy of Peter Lodoen

A village family sits in front of its brick dwelling to eat a morning meal.

Religion

Almost half of the Central African population holds traditional African religious beliefs, which include the idea of a supreme being. This god is worshiped from a distance, and its name is not spoken. Another age-old religious teaching is that those who have died remain part of the living community. The most sacred rites for people who hold traditional beliefs occur when young people are initiated into adulthood.

In addition to African teachings, Christian ideas have taken root in the Central African Republic. Christian missionaries arrived in the region at the end of the nineteenth century and established schools

Traditional rites of passage (change) are an important part of age-old African beliefs that many Central Africans follow.

A Christian preacher speaks to a crowd at a rural church. Unlike this minister, who is a Central African, most Christian leaders in the nation are from other countries.

Christian churches — such as this one near the Ubangi River — are located throughout the country.

and medical facilities. As a result, approximately 50 percent of the population is Christian. Half of this group is Roman Catholic, and the other half belongs to one of several Protestant groups.

About 1 percent of the people practice the Islamic religion, which was founded by the prophet Muhammad on the Arabian Peninsula in the seventh century A.D. Arab traders brought Islam to central Africa beginning in the sixteenth century.

Health

Most of the Central African Republic lacks modern medical facilities. Bangui is the only place that consistently has a full range of medical supplies on hand. The majority of hospital and medical personnel live and work in the capital. A few Christian medical outposts exist in rural areas, and the government has built small hospitals in large towns.

In addition to the lack of modern medical facilities, traditional African health practices, which use medicines made of herbs, have also declined in the region. Moreover, the population suffers from substandard diets, unsafe supplies of water, and poor sanitation facilities.

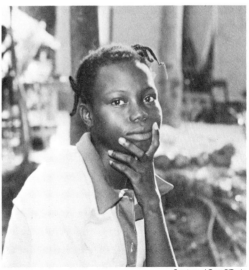

This young Central African has a life expectancy of 43 years, according to the 1988 statistics for citizens of his nation.

The region's infant mortality rate (the number of deaths among children younger than one year of age) is 148 deaths per 1,000 live births. This rate is among the highest in Africa. Only 16 percent of the country's people have access to safe water. The shortage of clean water accounts for many of the water-borne diseases—including several types of intestinal diseases—that afflict the population.

Other diseases that occur frequently in the region include anemia (a blood ailment), tuberculosis, hepatitis (inflammation of the liver), sleeping sickness (transmitted by tsetse fly bites), and acquired immune deficiency syndrome (AIDS). Health officials estimate that 5 percent of the nation's urban residents carry the AIDS virus.

Courtesy of Peter Lodoen

After surviving childhood diseases, Central Africans face other serious health threats as they grow older. Common ailments include tuberculosis and sleeping sickness.

Education

Until 1953 the French colonial government did not provide educational opportunities beyond the elementary level. Secondary education in the Central African Republic was only offered in schools established by Christian missionaries. Most public schools were poorly equipped and had few teachers. The first publicly funded high school —Collège Emil Gentil—was established in 1953, and its first class graduated in 1956.

After independence in 1960, the government of the Central African Republic spent more than 20 percent of its budget on education, and the number of schools and students increased rapidly. By the late

Courtesy of American Lutheran Church

Secondary school students file into their classroom in the early morning. One out of ten youths of high school age attends classes at the secondary level.

1980s over 60 percent of the Central African population had attended primary school, and almost 10 percent had received a secondary school education. At the same time, the literacy rate among Central Africans was 33 percent, which is about average among African nations.

The University of Bangui, founded by Jean-Bedel Bokassa, has operated on an irregular basis since it opened in 1967. In the late 1980s the university included a college of education, the University Institute of Mines and Geology, the National School of Administration, the School of Arts and Crafts, a medical school, and the National School of Agriculture. The university offers free instruction, and approximately 1 percent of the population gains admittance.

Many students from wealthy families pursue their studies in France. Sometimes well-educated instructors, who started working in the schools of the Central African Republic, transfer from teaching into government positions to gain higher pay and greater prestige. As a result, teachers with less skill and poorer training often must handle large classes. French is used as the language of instruction in all post-primary classes. This practice contributes to a high rate of failure among students because a majority of them are not fluent in French.

The Arts

Until the nineteenth century, craftspeople in the region produced many fine handmade items, such as decorative pottery, intricately woven mats, fine-tooled leather goods, musical instruments, and handsome textiles. The slave trade and the early years of colonization disrupted the expansion of crafts, however, and most of them disappeared. Even in the late 1980s, roughly woven mats and baskets, simple wooden utensils, and plain pottery were all that remained of traditional local handiwork. In recent years handicraft workers

Courtesy of Eliot Elisofon, Eliot Elisofon Archives, National Museum of African Art, Smithsonian Institution

Central African artisans paint murals of animals on many public buildings and occasionally on family dwellings.

Courtesy of Kristine S. Schubert

The image of these birds is composed from artfully arranged butterfly wings that are glued to paper.

A village craftsperson displays the figures that he has carved from ebony. The dark wood is harvested in a nearby rain-forest.

have begun producing unique designs and pictures made from butterfly wings glued to paper.

Central African musicians form dance bands in Bangui and in some regional towns. These bands use electronic equipment to play popular music from around the world. Many of the groups also perform original Central African music, which is characterized by sad, haunting vocals and a strong, rhythmic beat.

Few works of literature from Central Africa have been published, although collectors are slowly gathering the region's

Women from a village gather to pound dried cassava into flour. The women pick out the large chunks of cassava that need to be ground a second time.

Courtesy of American Lutheran Church

On market days, people come into the large towns to sell products they have made and to buy goods that they need. These open-air gatherings provide opportunities for socializing as well as for business.

traditional oral legends and folk stories from villagers who remember them. Pierre Makombo Bamboté is a well-known Central African author who has written a novel entitled *Princess Mandopa*. He also published *News of Bangui*, which is a collection of short stories.

Central African artists have produced both watercolor and oil paintings. The murals and canvasses of Jerome Ramedané depict scenes of African animal life, hunting parties, and daily village life. Similar works are often found on the walls of restaurants, bars, and other gathering places in Bangui and large villages.

Food

In the fertile river valleys in the south and west, farmers grow millet (a cereal grain) and cassava (a root crop) to provide food for the nation's inhabitants. A plant with strong stalks and a large head of grain, millet grows five to six feet tall. After workers harvest the crop and pound the grain in a large tub with a wooden hammer, millet can be made into porridge or fermented into a slightly alcoholic drink.

Cassavas measure from one to two feet in length and resemble potatoes. In the Central African Republic people often use cassavas to make a sour, doughlike loaf. Central Africans have developed a way of drying cassava. After workers soften the root by pounding it, they grate the cassavas and spread out the small pieces to dry in the sun. The final product is a coarse flour. Dried cassava stays fresh for weeks and is easy to transport.

The majority of Central Africans live on a meager diet of cassava, millet, beans, and maize. Wealthy urban dwellers, in contrast, often eat meat, fruit, vegetables, and imported French cheese.

This man rides a bicycle—one of the more dependable means of transportation in the Central African Republic. An inadequate system of roadways hinders the nation's economic growth.

4) The Economy

Although the Central African Republic contains a number of natural resources that have yet to be tapped, several factors have held back the country's economic development. The nation's lack of a seaport seriously hampers the flow of trade in and out of the country. Poor roads and the absence of railways also inhibit growth. Many of the nation's industrial developers come from other regions. Indeed, few profitable companies belong to Central Africans. Consequently, much of the territory's wealth flows to France, Belgium, and other foreign countries.

In the late 1980s, 85 percent of all Central Africans were subsistence farmers—that is, farmers who produce just enough to feed their families. Of nearly 150,000 Central Africans who earn wages, about 35,000 work in industry—mostly in food processing, in mineral refining, and in textile manufacturing. An additional 115,000 employees—the rest of the paid work force—have positions in the government or in service industries, including hospitals and schools.

The basis of the Central African economy is agriculture, which includes livestock raising and timber cutting as well as farming. Increased export revenue from coffee, cotton, timber, and tobacco was a goal of the French and has been an aim of all Central African governments since independence. The major food crops with high nutritional value—corn, millet, peanuts, rice, and sesame seeds—are produced in quantities that are too small to meet the country's dietary needs. Cassava, which is easily grown but of little nutritional value, is the mainstay of the national diet.

Diamonds are the country's major export, accounting for more than one-quarter of its foreign income. Those who seek quick profits rather than long-term development—that is, the government, foreign mining companies, and smugglers—have dominated the diamond market since the late 1960s.

Central African cattle are mostly zebus, hardy animals that have adapted to the heat and that are resistant to many tropical diseases.

Courtesy of Tom O'Toole

Courtesy of American Lutheran Church

Young men till the land with a small tractor, which greatly increases the agricultural productivity of their farm.

51

Photo by Barry Hewlett

Uprooted and discarded trees line an unpaved road in the Lobaye region. Many farmers are attempting to increase their acreages by clearing land in the thick rain-forests of the southwestern Central African Republic.

In many cases, hunting is more important to these farmers than cultivation. Much of the country's meat supply comes from wild game, and only occasionally will a family serve a domestic chicken or goat at a family meal.

Bananas grow in the rain-forest, and rice and maize are raised in the southern portion of the savanna. These crops—along with peanuts and millet planted in the northern area of the savanna—could form an adequate nutritional base for the country's rural population. Nevertheless, most people produce nutritionally inferior foods, such as cassava.

The transition from growing valuable foods to planting this starchy root began in the first decades of the twentieth century. French landowners used most of the farmable acreages to grow cotton, coffee, and tobacco, leaving infertile areas for Central African farmers. Because cassavas grow well even on poor land and need little care, Central Africans began planting more of this crop.

Agriculture

Agriculture is the major activity of at least 85 percent of the country's population—including a significant proportion of city dwellers. Yet agricultural goods represent less than one-third of the nation's yearly economic output. About 10 percent of the country's area is suitable for farming, but only about one-sixth of that land is farmed. Nonresident foreigners own large acreages of land, which they use mainly as hunting reserves. These holdings, though fertile, remain undeveloped.

Most Central Africans live in rural villages and cultivate temporary fields. They clear the land of trees and brush by using the slash-and-burn technique before planting crops. After just a few years, the soil becomes depleted of its nutrients, and the farmers move on to other areas, where they repeat the process.

Courtesy of American Lutheran Church

A Central African infant gazes at a display of green mangoes—a minor bonanza in this country where most people live on cassava, maize, millet, and beans.

Many Central Africans eat some form of cassava at almost every meal. Here, women spread grated cassavas to dry in the sunlight. Once dried, cassava can be kept for weeks.

The market in Bouar (population 51,000) bustles with commercial and social activity. Bouar's population dwindles during the growing and hunting seasons, when many people go to rural areas to gather food. When they return to town, residents frequent this trading place once again as a source of both goods and information.

Coffee trees still thrive near Mbaiki, although coffee bean production has fallen since the 1960s. The French introduced cotton and coffee to the region of the Central African Republic in the 1920s, and farmers are now developing additional export crops, such as sugarcane and oil palm trees.

Courtesy of Tom O'Toole

EXPORT CROPS

French plantation owners introduced the nation's two main export crops—coffee and cotton—in the 1920s. The small-scale producers of the 1980s have had difficulty increasing crop volumes because they have little money to spend on replacing out-dated equipment. As a result, production levels have fallen since the 1960s. Harvests are likely to continue diminishing, since the small amounts of aid that international agencies offer usually benefit owners of large plantations and rarely reach the average farmer. Farmers are slowly developing new export crops, however, including palm oil and sugarcane.

The rollers of this sugarcane press squeeze sap from the plant stalks and send the liquid into a trough. The juice is then boiled down and concentrated into granulated sugar and molasses. Refined sugar is one of the nation's export crops.

Courtesy of American Lutheran Church

54

Nomadic herders travel throughout much of the Central African Republic and neighboring countries in search of grazing land for their livestock. Since the mid-1970s, immigrants who fled drought conditions in Chad and Sudan have brought many cattle with them, doubling the number of livestock in the country. Assisted by the World Bank, the Central African government has begun to help migratory herders protect their animals from disease.

Goats and sheep roam freely in some areas of the Central African Republic. They scavenge for food, as do other livestock, such as chickens, guinea fowl, turkeys, ducks, and an occasional horse or donkey. Some Central Africans have started poultry-raising businesses near Bangui and other large towns.

Mining

Most of the mining activity in the Central African Republic centers on its diamond

Courtesy of Baptist Mid-Missions

Two young Central Africans stake down the hide of a game animal as they begin the tanning process, which turns animal skin into leather.

Courtesy of Peter Lodoen

Because most roads in the Central African Republic are unpaved, donkeys — which are able to travel through rough terrain — are among the most dependable means of transporting local goods.

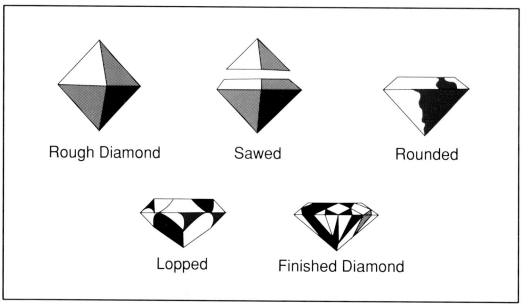

Diamonds are the hardest substance in the world. As a result, cutting gem-quality diamonds – using tools made with lower-grade diamonds – is a lengthy process that is accomplished in stages.

deposits, which are located in the western part of the country in a triangular region between Carnot, Berbérati, and Boda. Miners have extracted diamonds for about 60 years from the sandstone found near Carnot. Beginning in the late 1970s, new areas along the Bangui-Kette River also yielded a large supply of gem-quality diamonds.

The diamond industry uses an open-pit technique, in which miners remove dirt and rock from the surface of a strip of land as they search for diamonds. Miners often work in small groups during the dry season and return each year to their previously established pits.

Production and export levels rise and fall, depending upon the agreements between the government and foreign diamond companies, which regulate the market. Most diamonds are exported in raw, uncut form to Belgium and Israel for processing. A government marketing organization in Bangui maintains a local cutting operation. Smugglers take many diamonds out of the country, and some reports from international banks suggest that these illegal exporters make more money than the diamond companies do.

Since the mid-twentieth century, estimates have indicated that the Central African Republic might gain large profits if it were to tap more of its underground resources. But geologists in search of oil have found no major deposits, and prospecting miners have discovered only small amounts of gold and uranium.

Industry

Concentrated almost entirely in Bangui, the main manufacturing businesses in the Central African Republic include furniture workshops, soap factories, food and beverage processing plants, and textile mills. The government encourages international investment and uses funds from foreign lenders to support many firms. These include a slaughterhouse, a coffee-roasting plant, a record factory, and a clothes manufacturer. In the 1980s over 200 private businesses operated in the country.

Workers build a new high school in Baboua in the western part of the Central African Republic. Many construction materials must be imported, which makes new buildings expensive.

Courtesy of American Lutheran Church

The Central African Republic has several small food-processing plants that extract oils from sesame seeds, peanuts, and palm nuts. Ginneries, which separate raw cotton from its seeds, are well established in Berbérati and other regional towns. Workers then spin the cotton and send the yarns and threads to a textile mill in Bangui, where five million yards of cloth are produced each year.

Forestry and Fishing

Forests cover more than 5 percent of the nation's territory in the southwestern Central African Republic. Transportation difficulties, however, prevent profitable harvest of this natural resource. Moving timber to an export dock is an expensive challenge in a landlocked country.

About a dozen French, Swiss, Romanian, and Yugoslavian firms—some working

Courtesy of Ministry of Information, Central African Republic

Despite transportation difficulties, French, Swiss, Romanian, and Yugoslavian firms continue to cut timber in the Central African Republic. Because these companies do not plant new trees, forest conservation has become a critical issue for the Central African Republic.

A Gbaya woman who lives near Baboua manages to carry a load of wood—the nation's most common source of fuel—as well as her child and a pan.

on joint projects with the government—cut timber, but they have made no attempt to reforest the land. As a result, the forests of the Central African Republic, like those in much of the tropical world, are steadily shrinking. Once an area has been completely cleared of trees, it lies barren because tropical forests do not regrow without replanting. In dry savanna areas, firewood and building materials are becoming scarce. All these factors make forest conservation a critical concern for officials in the Central African Republic.

Fishing productivity increased in the Central African Republic during the early 1980s. In the first half of the decade the freshwater catch improved by 10 percent. Much of this increase is due to the development of fish breeding in ponds. The catch is harvested when the fish are grown.

Courtesy of American Lutheran Church

These men fish using traps placed in the Mbéré River. The nation's freshwater catch increased by 10 percent in the 1980s.

Courtesy of United Nations

Fishermen use modern techniques to increase their catches at this fishing center near Bangui. After netting fish in the center's ponds, the fishermen sell their daily take in nearby villages.

Many river travelers use canoes that are formed by burning out the inside of large logs. The burning of the wood is carefully controlled so that the part of the log that makes up the canoe is not damaged.

Transportation

The Central African Republic, like many other equatorial African countries, began to change its basic form of transportation during the twentieth century. The nation has replaced large river-going canoes with river barges, motor vehicles, and aircraft.

By the 1980s several international airlines were landing at the modern Bangui-Mpoko Airport.

The nation's inland network of waterways includes over 7,000 miles of navigable rivers. Barge traffic on the Ubangi and Zaire rivers handles 75 percent of the

The road from Carnot to Bouar is typical of many of the unpaved roads in the nation. After the rainy season begins, the bed of the roadway is often washed away.

Waterfalls make it difficult to use rivers as transport routes. But falls do offer the possibility of hydroelectric power.

nation's international trade, even though large barges cannot travel on the Ubangi River during the dry season. Poor navigational conditions, a shortage of functional barges, and ineffective management caused a decline in river shipping in the 1980s. Nevertheless, barges remain the cheapest means of moving bulk goods such as timber and cotton.

The Central African Republic has no seaports, and consequently its imports and exports must travel great distances overland before passing through the docks at Pointe Noire in Congo and Douala in Cameroon. Because transportation through these shipping centers is costly, the price of all goods going into or out of the country is high.

The Central African Republic has no railroads, and its 13,300-mile network of roads has only 400 miles of paved surface. The Trans-African Highway, however—being

The Central African Republic depends on imports for farm equipment, automobiles, trucks, and other large machines.

built from Lagos in Nigeria to Mombasa in Kenya—will pass through Bangui. In addition, a number of roads that will intersect with that highway's route in the Central African Republic are being upgraded. Another major roadway—which starts in the Central African Republic and which passes through Cameroon to the Atlantic coast—is especially important. Many importers and exporters prefer to take their goods over this land route than to use riverways for transport.

Future Challenges

Members of a number of rival ethnic groups, Central Africans have yet to achieve national unity. Increased local participation in a democratic system of government, however, may help these diverse peoples to overcome their differences. Many Central Africans urge the country's leaders to put an end to government corruption—especially by limiting the number of government employees and by stopping the misuse of government funds.

Visitors trample the grass near a fallen statue of Jean-Bedel Bokassa. Corrupt leadership during Bokassa's years in power has left the Central African Republic economically and politically unstable.

If the Central African Republic can end the corruption that drains its financial resources, the nation's economic life may improve. The development of transportation routes that connect this landlocked country to world markets could also enrich the economy.

Because agriculture is the main activity of the work force, better farming techniques and improved crop management are important goals. If the nation achieves these agricultural aims, more nutritious food and larger export crops are likely to result. Many people within the nation hope to increase the number of locally owned businesses and to decrease the country's reliance on foreign investment. The Central African Republic's response to these political and economic challenges will determine the future of the nation.

Central Africans gather around a drummer to keep time with his music. Overcoming interethnic conflicts and increasing democratic participation in government are important challenges for the Central African Republic.

Courtesy of American Lutheran Church

Index